# Granny Square Blankets

*Granny Square Blanket Patterns to Crochet*

Copyright © 2023

All rights reserved.

### DEDICATION

# Contents

# Strawberry Granny Square

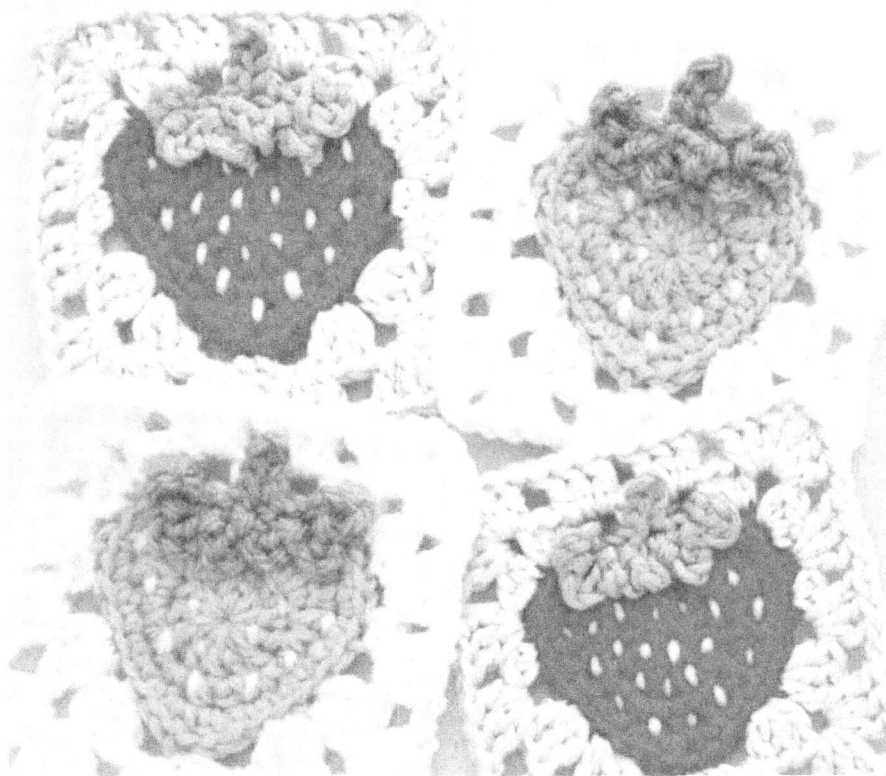

## MATERIALS

4.5-mm (7 USA, 7 UK) Crochet Hook

Aran (4, Medium) Yarn

Tapestry Needle

## YARN

Paintbox Yarns Wool Mix Aran (1) and Paintbox Yarns Simply Aran (2) in the following colors:

A – (1), Blush Pink (853)

B – (2), Lime Green (228)

C – (2), Champagne White (202)

Feel free to use any yarn with the appropriate hook.

## SIZE

4" (10 cm)

## GAUGE

4 rounds of a granny square in 4" (10 cm).

## ABBREVIATIONS (US TERMS)

BLO – Back Loop Only

Ch – Chain

Hdc – Half Double Crochet

Dc – Double Crochet

Inc – Increase

MC – Magic Circle

RS – Right Side

Sc – Single Crochet

Sk – Skip

Sp – Space

Sl St – Slip Stitch

St – Stitch

Yo – Yarn Over

## SPECIAL STITCHES

Back Loop Only (BLO)

Increase (Inc)

One increase consists of 2 sts worked in the same indicated st. The pattern indicates when to make a sc, hdc, dc, or tr inc.

Magic Circle (MC)

## PATTERN NOTES

If the pattern says "sc 2", you need to sc 1 in each of the next 2 sts.

(…) – Repeat the instructions within brackets for the indicated number of times.

*… – Repeat the instructions from * for the indicated number of times.

[…] – Crochet the instructions within brackets all in the same indicated st.

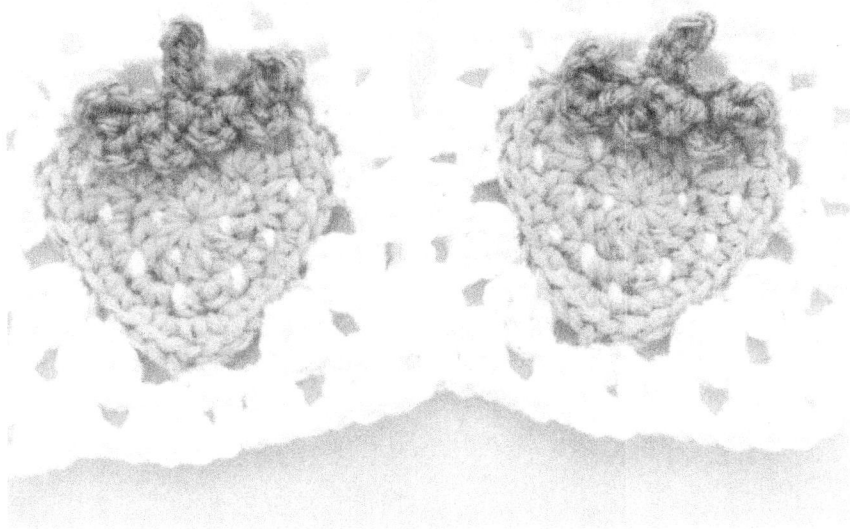

PATTERN

STRAWBERRY

Using A, make a MC.


Round 1. Ch 2 (does not count as a st here and throughout), dc 12 in

MC, join with a sl st in first dc. (12 sts)

Round 2. Ch 1 (does not count as a st here and throughout), hdc 1 in first st, [dc 4], [hdc 1, sc 1], sc 1, sc inc 1, hdc 2, sc inc 1, sc 1, [sc 1, hdc 1], [dc 4], hdc 1, join with a sl st in first hdc. (22 sts)

Round 3. Ch 1, sc 2, sc inc 3, sc 5, [sc 1, hdc 1], ch 1 (bottom of strawberry!), [hdc 1, sc 1], sc 5, sc inc 3, sc 2, join with a sl st in first sc. (31 sts, 1 ch)

Fasten off A.

SQUARING

RS facing, hold your strawberry with the bottom up, and join C in BLO of ch-1 of round 3.

Round 4. BLO sc 1 in same st as joining, ch 1, sk 3, [BLO dc 3] in next st, ch 2, [BLO dc 3] in next, ch 1, sk 2, BLO sc inc 1, ch 1, sk 2, [BLO sc 2, BLO hdc 1] in next st, ch 2, [BLO hdc 3] in next st, ch 1, sk 2, BLO hdc 2, ch 1, sk 2, [BLO hdc 3] in next st, ch 2, [BLO hdc 1, BLO sc 2] in next, ch 1, sk 2, BLO sc inc 1, ch 1, sk 2, [BLO dc 3] in next st, ch 2, [BLO dc 3] in next, ch 1, sk 3, BLO sc 1 in beginning ch-1, join with a sl st in first sc.

Round 5. Sl st in next ch-1 sp and ch 2 (counts as the post of a dc), [dc 2] in same ch-1 sp, ch 1, *[dc 3, ch 2, dc 3] in next ch-2 sp, ch 1, ([dc 3] in next ch-1 sp, ch 1) twice. Repeat from * 3 times. [Dc 3, ch 2, dc 3] in last ch-2 sp, ch 1, [dc 3] in next ch-1 sp, ch 1, join with a sl st in first dc (and not into initial ch-2!).

Fasten off and weave in all your ends.

## LEAVES

RS facing and holding your square with the bottom of the strawberry down, join B in the st on round 3 next to the top, right corner, or left corner if you are left-handed.

Row 1. Ch 1 (counts as a sl st), FLO sl st 2, ch 4, sl st 1 in second ch from hook, sl st 2, FLO sl st 1 in next st on round 3, FLO sl st 2. (6 sl sts, 1 stem)

Row 2. Ch 4, tilt your square so that you can crochet on the lower loops on the sl sts you made in row 1.

Sl st in the lower loop of first sl st, (ch 4, sl st in the lower loop of next sl st) 5 times.

Fasten off and weave in your ends.

FINISHING

With a length of C, embroider the seed of the strawberry.

Fasten off and weave in all your ends.

# Puff Flower Granny Square Blanket

Skill Level: Intermediate

Measurements: 6" x 6"


Supplies:

Yarn: Red Heart Super Saver Worsted Weight #4 (5 Colors)

Hook: 5.0 mm [US H]

Stitch Markers – quantity (1)

Yarn needle

Gauge: Finished square through Round 6 = 6 inches

Abbreviations:

beg – beginning

ch – chain

dc – double crochet

sc – single crochet

sl st – slip stitch

sp(s) – space(s)

st(s) – stitch(es)

tr – treble crochet

# Granny Square Blankets

Special Stitches & Placement:

Front Post Treble – fptr: yo 2x, insert hook from front to back, around stitch, and to front, yo, pull through, 4 loops on hook,[yo, pull through 2 loops on hook] 3x.

Popcorn – pc: 4 dc in same st, remove hook from loop, insert hook front to back through top of first dc st, put loop back on hook, pull through first st. (1 pc).

Reverse Single Crochet – rsc: insert hook in previous st, yo, pull up loop, yo, pull through both loops on hook. (1 rsc made).

Standing Double Crochet – sdc: with slip knot on hook, yo, insert hook into designated stitch, yo, pull through, 3 loops on hook, [yo, pull through 2 loops on hook] 2x.

Notes:

1. Ch 4 count as a dc.

2. Weave in ends after each round.

3. Written in US terminology

4. Instructions are written with sdc to begin most rounds OR another option to start each round with ch3 in place of sdc.

5. If you're using the standing stitches at the beginning of the round, you will end the round by placing a slip stitch to the beginning standing stitch (instead of a sl st to top of beginning ch-3 stitch).

Instructions:

Notes:

Make 1 complete square Rounds 1-6, set aside.

Make 14 squares Rounds 1-5. See 1 Sided Join-As-You-Go instructions below for Round 6 to complete.

Make 45 squares Rounds 1-5. See 2 Sided Join-As-You-Go instructions below for Round 6 to complete.

Color A – Place slip knot on hook.

Round 1: Ch 4 (counts as 1 dc), 11 dc in 1st ch, join with sl st to top of ch 3. (12 dc). End off yarn.

Color B – Place slip knot on hook, begin in any space between stitches.

Round 2: 1 sdc, 3 dc in same st, *sk 2 sts, 4 dc in next st, repeat from *, join with sl st to beg sdc. (24 dc). End off yarn.

Color C – Place slip knot on hook, begin in any stitch.

Round 3: 1 sdc, ch 1, *1 dc in next st, ch1, repeat from *, join with sl st to beg sdc. (24 dc, 24 ch-1 sps). Drop loop off hook, place stitch marker in loop.

Note: Round 4 is worked on top of Round 3 to make the popcorn stitches. Use surface crochet to work around the dc sts from Round 3.

Color D – Place slip knot on hook, begin around any dc stitch.

Round 4: 1 sdc, 3 dc around same st, close pc st, *ch 3 loosely, skip 1 dc, 1 pc around next dc, repeat from *, end with ch 3 loosely, sl st to ch 1 after 1st pc. (12 pc). End off yarn. It will curl up like a little bowl, this is correct.

Color C – Remove stitch marker from loop, place loop back on hook.

Notes:

Work into Round 3.

Make 4 corners in this round.

Alternate working behind the pc sts and in front of the pc sts, moving the ch 3, and pc sts out of the way.

Round 5: Ch 4 (counts as 1 tr) 1 tr in next sp to left of same pc, *3 fptr between pc sts around skipped dc st, [1 tr in next sp behind pc on right, 1 tr in sp behind pc on left, 1 fptr between pc sts around next dc st] 2x, 1 tr in next sp behind pc on right, 1 tr in next sp behind pc on left, repeat from *, end with 1 fptr between pc sts around dc st, sl st to top of beg Ch 4. (24 tr, 8 fptr, 4 corners with 3 fptr in each one (total of 12 fptr)).

Color E – Place slip knot on hook, begin in 1st space of any corner.

Round 6: 1 sdc, 2 dc in same sp, ch 5, 3 dc in next corner sp, *skip 2 sts, 3 dc in next st, [skip 3 sts, 3 dc in next st] 2x, skip 2 sts, 3 dc in 1st corner sp, ch 5, 3 dc in next corner sp, repeat from *, end with skip 2 sts, 3 dc in next st, [skip 3 sts, 3 dc in next st] 2x, sl st to beg dc. (60 dc, 4 ch-5 loops).

Square with 1 sided join: (Make 14)

Repeat Rounds 1-5 above.

Place WS facing of adjacent square, RS facing of current square. Work in current square unless specified to work in adjacent square.

Begin in 1st space of any corner on current square.

Round 6: 1 sdc, 2 dc in same sp, ch 2, join with sl st to 3rd ch of adjacent square, ch 2, 3 dc in next corner sp, sl st to 3rd dc of adjacent square, skip 2 sts, 3 dc in next st, sl st to 3rd dc of adjacent square, [skip 3 sts, 3 dc in next st, sl st to 3rd dc of adjacent square] 2x, skip 2 sts, 3 dc in 1st corner sp, ch 2, join with sl st to 3rd ch of adjacent square, ch 2, 3 dc in next corner sp, *skip 2 sts, 3 dc in next st, [skip 3 sts, 3 dc in next st] 2x, skip 2 sts, 3 dc in 1st corner sp, ch 5, 3 dc in next corner sp, repeat from *, end with skip 2 sts, 3 dc in next st, [skip 3 sts, 3 dc in next st] 2x, sl st to beg dc. (60 dc, 2 ch-5 loops, 6 sl sts).

Granny Square Blankets

Square with 2 sided join:  (Make 45)

Repeat Rounds 1-5 above.

Place WS facing of adjacent square, RS facing of current square. Work in current square unless specified to work in adjacent square.

Begin in 1st space of any corner on current square.

Round 6: 1 sdc, 2 dc in same sp, ch 2,  join with sl st to 3rd ch of adjacent square, ch 2, 3 dc in next corner sp, *sl st to 3rd dc of adjacent square, skip 2 sts, 3 dc in next st, sl st to 3rd dc of adjacent square, [skip 3 sts, 3 dc in next st, sl st to 3rd dc of adjacent square] 2x, skip 2 sts, 3 dc in 1st corner sp, ch 2, join with sl st to 3rd ch of adjacent square, ch 2, 3 dc in next corner sp, repeat from * 1 more time; skip 2 sts, 3 dc in next st, [skip 3 sts, 3 dc in next st] 2x, skip 2 sts, 3 dc in 1st corner sp, ch 5, 3 dc in next corner sp, skip 2 sts, 3 dc in next st, [skip 3 sts, 3 dc in next st] 2x, end with sl st to beg dc. (60 dc, 1 ch-5 loop,

11 sl sts).

Border:

Color E –begin in any corner space.

Round 1: 1 sdc, 2 dc in same sp, ch 2, 3 dc in same sp, *1 dc in each st to next corner [3 dc, ch 2, 3 dc], repeat from *, end with 1 dc in each st across, sl st to beg dc.

Round 2: Ch 1, 1 sc in same st, ch 1, 1 sc in same st, *1 sc in each st to next corner [1sc, ch 1, 1 sc}, repeat from *, end with 1 sc in each st across, sl st to beg sc.

Round 3: Ch 1, *1 rsc in next st, skip 1 st, 1 rsc in next st, repeat * around, end with sl st to beg rsc. End off yarn, weave in ends.

Color C –begin in any stitch, work around top of dc from Round 1 of border.

Round 4: 1 sl st around top of dc, *ch 4, skip 2 sts, 1 sl st around next st, repeat from *, end with ch 4, sl st to beg sl st. End off yarn, weave in ends.

# Granny's Little Girl Crochet Blanket

Measure: approx 70 x 100 cm / 27½"x39½"

Materials: DROPS ALPACA from Garnstudio

350 g color no 0100, off-white

50 g color no 2110, wheat

50 g color no 2923, goldenrod

50 g color no 2915, orange

50 g color no 2921, pink

50 g color no 3140, light pink

50 g color no 0618, light beige mix

50 g color no 7300, lime

50 g color no 2917, turquoise

50 g color no 2918, dark turquoise

DROPS CROCHET HOOK size 5 mm / H/8 – or size needed to get 1 square to measure approx 12 x 12 cm / 4¾" x 4¾".

BLANKET:

TIP: When crocheting the sl st at the end of a round, do it with the color of next round.

## COLORS OF SQUARES:

A (make 3): Beg + round 1 = light pink, round 2 = goldenrod, round 3 = wheat, round 4 and 5 = off-white.

B (make 5): Beg + round 1 = wheat, round 2 = dark turquoise, round 3 = lime, round 4 and 5 = off-white.

C (make 5): Beg + round 1 = orange, round 2 = light pink, round 3 = lime, round 4 and 5 = off-white.

D (make 3): Beg + round 1 = turquoise, round 2 = pink, round 3 = light beige mix, round 4 and 5 = off-white.

E (make 4): Beg + round 1 = wheat, round 2 = dark turquoise, round 3 = turquoise, round 4 and 5 = off-white.

F (make 5): Beg + round 1 = orange, round 2 = turquoise, round 3 = light pink, round 4 and 5 = off-white.

G (make 3): Beg + round 1 = wheat, round 2 = goldenrod, round 3 = pink, round 4 and 5 = off-white.

H (make 5): Beg + round 1 = goldenrod, round 2 = light pink, round 3 = light beige mix, round 4 and 5 = off-white.

I (make 2): Beg + round 1 = light beige mix, round 2 = lime, round 3 = pink, round 4 and 5 = off-white.

# Granny Square Blankets

= a total of 35 squares.

## SQUARE:

Ch 6 with 2 strands Alpaca and hook size 5 mm / H/8 and form a ring with 1 sl st in first ch.

ROUND 1: ch 3, 15 dc in ring, finish with 1 sl st in 3rd ch from beg of round = 16 dc, turn piece.

ROUND 2: ch 3, 2 dc in first dc, * ch 2, skip 1 dc, 3 dc in next dc *, repeat from *-* a total of 7 times and finish with ch 2 and 1 sl st in 3rd ch from beg of round = 8 dc-groups, turn piece.

ROUND 3: ch 3, 1 dc in first ch-loop, ch 1, 2 dc in the same ch-loop, * ch 1, 2 dc in next ch-loop, ch 1, 2 dc in the same ch-loop *, repeat from *-* a total of 7 times and finish with ch 1 and 1 sl st in 3rd ch from beg of round, turn piece = 8 dc-groups.

ROUND 4: ch 2, 2 hdc in first ch-loop, ch 1, * 3 dc in next ch-loop, ch 3, 3 dc in next ch-loop, ch 1, 3 hdc in next ch-loop, ch 1, 3 hdc in next ch-loop, ch 1 *, repeat from *-* a total of 3 times, 3 dc in next ch-loop, ch 3, 3 dc in next ch-loop, ch 1, 3 hdc in next ch-loop, ch 1 and finish with 1 sl st in 2nd ch from beg of round, turn piece.

ROUND 5: Crochet sl sts to the middle of ch-loop, * ch 2, 1 sc in next ch-loop, ch 2, in next ch-loop crochet: 1 hdc, 2 dc, ch 3, 2 dc and 1 hdc (= corner), ch 2, 1 sc in next ch-loop, ch 2, 1 sc in next ch-loop *, repeat from *-* a total of 3 times, ch 2, 1 sc in next ch-loop, ch 2, in next ch-loop crochet: 1 hdc, 2 dc, ch 3, 2 dc and 1 hdc (= corner), ch 2, 1 sc in next ch-loop, ch 2, finish with 1 sl st in sl st from beg of round.

ASSEMBLY:

Place squares with 5 squares horizontally and 7 squares vertically – see photo for color combination. Crochet squares tog with 2 strands off-white Alpaca and hook size 5 mm / H/8 – beg crochet squares horizontally, place 2 squares on top of each other WS towards WS and crochet tog through both layers as follows (also see fig.1): 1 sc in first ch-loop (= corner) on first square, ch 2, 1 sc in corner on second square, * ch 3, 1 sc in next ch-loop on first square, ch 2, 1 sc in next ch-loop on second square *, repeat from *-* a total of 4 times, ch 3, 1 sc in last ch-loop (= corner) on first square, ch 2, 1 sc in last ch-loop (= corner) on second square, ch 3, 1 sc in corner of third square, ch 2, 1 sc in corner of fourth square etc across the row until 5 squares have been crochet tog. Crochet the other rows of squares tog 5 by 5. When all squares have been crochet tog horizontally crochet the rows tog vertically in the same way.

CROCHET BORDER:

Crochet a border round the whole blanket with hook size 5 mm / H/8 and 2 strands off-white Alpaca as follows:

ROUND 1 (crochet from WS): Crochet 3 dc in each ch-loop and crochet ch 2 between each dc-group (also crochet 1 dc-group in each transition between squares). In each corner crochet 3 dc, ch 3 and 3 dc in the same ch-loop, turn piece.

ROUND 2: Crochet 1 sc in first ch-loop, * ch 3, 1 dc in the first of the ch 3, 1 sc in next ch-loop *, repeat from *-*. NOTE: In each corner crochet 1 extra loop to make the corner sit nicely.

# Big And Small Granny Square

Materials

Crochet Hook:  4mm or size needed to achieve gauge

Yarn: DK weight yarn in ten colours, 295m for each of eight colours (C-J), 590m in a nineth colour (B) and 1180m of a joining colour (A).

# Granny Square Blankets

The sample uses Stylecraft Special DK (100% Acrylic) in:

Cream (A) – (400g/1180m),

Raspberry (B) – (200g/590m)

Grey (C) – (100g/295m),

Duck Egg (D) – (100g/295m),

Toy (E) – (100g/295m)

Grape (F) – (100g/295m)

Parma Violet (G) – (100g/295m)

Mushroom (H) – (100g/295m)

Blush (I) – (100g/295m)

Wisteria (J) – (100g/295m)

You can purchase this yarn here.

Notions:    Scissors

Needle to weave in ends

Finished size:    Approximately 130cm x 130cm

# Granny Square Blankets

Skill Level: Suitable for beginners

Gauge:    4 rounds in pattern = 8.5cm x 8.5cm, adjust hook size as necessary  Gauge is not critical for this project, but may affect yarn quantities

Abbreviations/Crochet terminology:

UK terms are used throughout.

ss      slip stitch

tr      treble crochet

htc     half treble crochet

dc double crochet

ch      chain

beg-ch beginning chain

*to*    instructions between asterisks will be repeated as specified

Instructions

The pattern is based on the traditional Granny Square. There are two different sizes of Granny Squares to make (small and large). The Granny Squares are rotated in the blanket so that the corners are pointing in the north, south, east and west positions. This means that there are also some Half Granny Squares (small and large) and Quarter Granny Squares to make. The diagram below show you how this works.

KEY

Large Granny Square (joining round in yarn A)

Small Granny Square (joining round in yarn A)

Small Granny Square (joining round in yarn B)

Half Small Granny Square (joining round in yarn B)

Quarter Large Granny Square (joining round in yarn A)

Half Large Granny Square (joining round in yarn A)

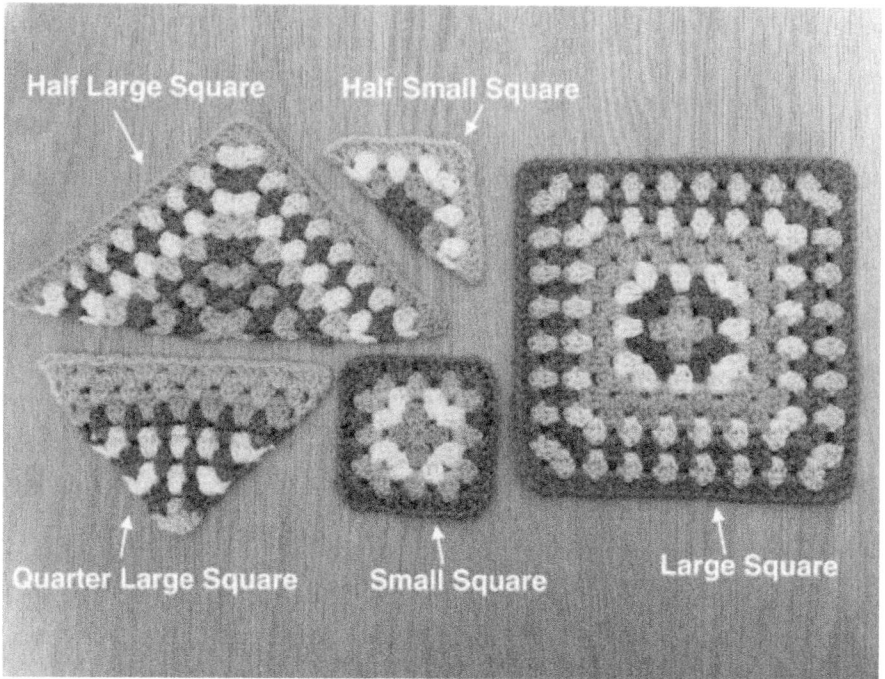

Half Large Square    Half Small Square

Quarter Large Square    Small Square    Large Square

Notes on the Granny Squares

The Granny Square uses groups of treble crochet to form 'treble clusters'. It is a really simple technique and suitable for a beginner. There are many different ways to make a Granny Square – this pattern has one chain stitch in each corner. The pattern also suggests you turn the work over after each round, and to start a new colour in a different corner each time. The half and quarter granny squares are also worked using these same principles.

Granny Square Blankets

In this project all of the pieces are joined together using the join-as-you-go method, whilst working the final round on each piece.

Small Granny Squares and the Small Half Granny Squares have a total of 5 rounds, including the join-as-you-go round, so in the first instance these need to made up to the 4th round and the 5th round will be added later when you join.

Large Granny Squares, Large Half Granny Squares, and the Quarter Granny Squares have a total of 10 rounds, including the join-as-you-go round, so in the first instance these need to made up to the 9th round and the 10th round will be added later when you join.

Small Granny Squares

You will need to make 84. Work 4 rounds of the Granny Square pattern below (you will join on the 5th round using the join-as-you method of joining – explained later). Make 72 of these so that cream (A) is not on the 4th round (as these are going to be joined using cream (A)), and make 12 of these ensuring that raspberry (B) is not on the

4th round (as these are joined using Raspberry).

Large Granny Squares

You will need to make 13 of the Large Granny Squares. Work 9 rounds of the Granny Square pattern (you will join on the 10th round using the join-as-you method of joining – explained later). Make all of these so that cream (A) is not on the 9th round, as these are going to be joined using cream (A).

## Half Small Granny Squares

You will need to make 12 small Half Granny Squares. Work up to the 4th round, ensuring that the final round is not yarn B (raspberry) as this will be the joining colour on round 5.

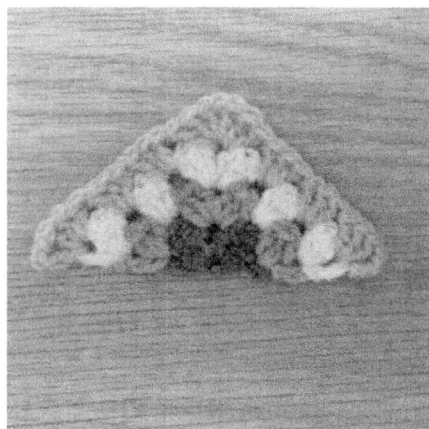

## Half Large Granny Squares

You will need to make 8 large Half Granny Squares. Work up to the 9th round, ensuring that the final round is not yarn A (cream) as this will be the joining colour on round 10.

Quarter Granny Squares

You will need to make 4 Quarter Granny Squares. You will need to make these with 9 rounds. Make sure that these do not have cream (yarn A) as the 9th round, as this will be used when joining on the 10th round.

## Arrangement of Pieces

Arrange your pieces as follows. You can ensure that there is a good balance of colours across your work.

## Joining the Pieces

Each piece made will be joined to the adjacent pieces whilst working the final round of each piece. This meant that all of the pieces that had the final round worked in Cream (yarn A) were all joined first.

The join-as-you-go joining method is explained here.

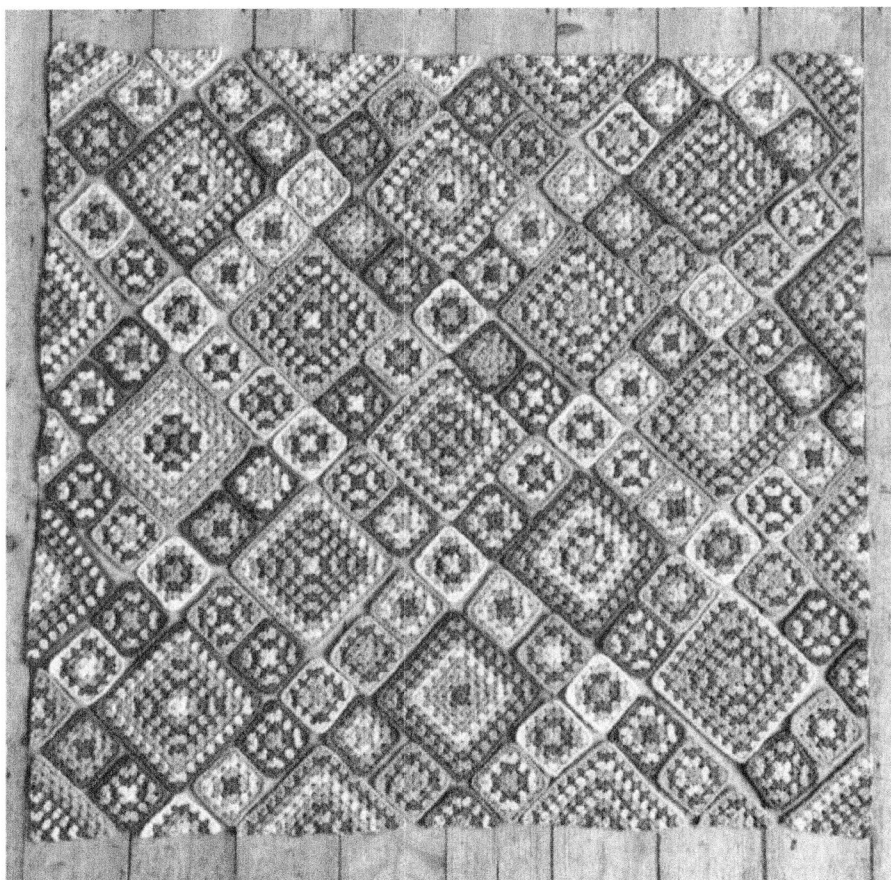

Border

The border is a very simple, 3 round border worked all in Raspberry (yarn B).

Border Round 1:

Pull up a loop in any corner using Yarn B (Raspberry), ch1 and work a dc around the whole blanket, ensuring that each dc is evenly spaced. When you reach a corner work 3dc. On reaching back at the start, work 3dc in the corner and then ss in the ch1 you worked at the start. DO NOT fasten off.

Border Round 2:

Ch2 (counts as 1HTC), work one HTC in each stitch around the blanket, working 3HTC in each corner. One reaching the corner where you started work 3HTC and ss in the ch2 worked at the start of the round. DO NOT fasten off.

Border Round 3:

Ch3 (counts as 1tr), work 1tr in between each of the HTC stitches you worked in the previous round, working [3tr, ch1, 3tr] in each corner. When you reach the corner at the start of the round, work [3tr, ch1, 3tr] in the final corner and ss into the ch3 worked at the start. Fasten off and weave in all ends.

# Grandma's Hugs Crochet Blanket

SIZE:

Width approx. = 90 cm. Length = 124 cm.

1 square measures approx. 34 x 34 cm.

MATERIALS:

DROPS AIR from Garnstudio (belongs to yarn group C)

200 g colour 01, off white

100 g colour 26, beige

100 g colour 33, pink sand

50 g colour 02, wheat

50 g colour 32, blush

CROCHET HOOK:

DROPS CROCHET HOOK SIZE 5 MM.

CROCHET TENSION:

14 treble crochets in width and 8.5 rows in height = 10 cm.

Hook size is only a guide. If you get too many stitches on 10 cm, change to a larger hook size. If you get too few stitches on 10 cm, change to a smaller hook size.

PATTERN:

See diagrams A.1 to A.7.

COLOURS SQUARE (A.1 to A.3):

CAST ON and ROUND 1: off white

ROUND 2: pink sand

ROUND 3: blush

ROUND 4: wheat

ROUND 5: beige

ROUND 6: off white

ROUND 7: pink sand

ROUND 8: off white

COLOURS EDGE (A.4 to A.6):

ROUND 1: off white

ROUND 2: wheat

ROUND 3: beige

ROUND 4: off white

ROUND 5: pink sand

ROUND 6: off white

ROUND 7: blush

ROUND 8: pink sand

ROUND 9: off white

## COLOUR-CHANGE TIP:

When changing colour work as follows: Work the last stitch on the round with the old colour, but wait with the final yarn over and pull-through, change to the next colour and work the yarn over and pull-through, then continue as shown in the diagram

## BLANKET – SHORT OVERVIEW OF THE PIECE:

The blanket is made up of 6 squares which are sewn together, 2 squares in width, 3 squares in length. An edge is worked around the whole blanket.

1 SQUARE:

Read COLOURS SQUARE in explanations above. Start with hook size 5 mm and colour off white in DROPS Air. Work 5 chain stitches and form them into a ring with 1 slip stitch in the first chain stitch.

Read COLOUR-CHANGE TIP, and work diagram A.1 (circle). REMEMBER THE CROCHET TENSION! When A.1 has been completed, continue as follows: Work A.2 (= beginning and end of the round), A.3 four times around the circle.

When A.2 and A.3 are finished, cut and fasten the strands.

Work 6 squares.

ASSEMBLY:

Lay the squares out with 2 squares in width and 3 squares in length – see A.7. NOTE: Make sure the square marked with a black star lies so the end of the round is towards the outside edge. The star marks the start of the edge to be worked later. Sew the squares together edge to edge so the seam is flat. Cut and fasten the strands.

EDGE:

Read COLOURS EDGE in the explanations above. Start in the stitch marked with a star in A.2. Work A.4 in this stitch, then A.5 three times, work A.6 in the corner, work A.5 to the next corner – NOTE: In each transition between 2 squares work 1 chain stitch, 2 treble crochets around the corner chain-space on the first square, 1 chain stitch, 2 treble crochets around the corner chain-space on the second square. Continue like this around the whole blanket.

When A.4 to A.6 are finished, cut and fasten the strands.

# Easy Crochet Granny Blanket

Difficulty LevelEasy

Crochet HookI/9 or 5.5 mm hook

Crochet Gauge12 sc and 14 rows = 4" [10 cm]

# Granny Square Blankets

Finished SizeApprox 56" x 60"

Materials List

Bernat® Crushed Velvet™ (10.5 oz/300 g; 315 yds/288 m)

Contrast A Navy (16011) - 2 balls

Contrast B White (16007) - 2 balls

Size U.S. I/9 (5.5 mm) crochet hook or size needed to obtain gauge.

Instructions

1st rnd: (RS). 2 dc in 4th ch from hook (counts as 3 dc). (Ch 1. Skip next 3 ch. 3 dc in next ch) twice. Ch 1. Skip next 3 ch. [(3 dc. Ch 3) twice. 3 dc] all in last ch. Working along other side of foundation ch, (Ch 1. Skip next 3 ch. 3 dc in next ch) twice. Ch 1. Skip next 3 dc. (3 dc. Ch 3) twice in last ch. Join with sl st to 3rd ch of beg ch.

2nd rnd: Sl st in each of next 2 dc and ch-1 sp. Ch 3 (counts as dc). 2 dc in same sp as last sl st. (Ch 1. 3 dc in next ch-1 sp) twice. (Ch 1. 3 dc. Ch 3. 3 dc in next ch-1 sp) twice. (Ch 1. 3 dc in next ch-1 sp) 3 times. Ch 1. (3 dc. Ch 3. 3 dc) in each of next 2 ch-3 sps. Ch 1. Join B with sl st to top of ch 3.

3rd rnd: With B, sl st in each of next 2 dc and ch-1 sp. Ch 3 (counts as dc). 2 dc in same sp as last sl st. (Ch 1. 3 dc in next ch-1 sp) twice. Ch 1. (3 dc. Ch 3. 3 dc) in next corner ch-3 sp. Ch 1. 3 dc in next ch-1 sp. (3 dc. Ch 3. 3 dc) in next corner ch-3 sp. (Ch 1. 3 dc in next ch-1 sp) 4 times. Ch 1. (3 dc. Ch 3. 3 dc) in next ch-3 sp. Ch 1. 3 dc in next ch-1 sp. Ch 1. (3 dc. Ch 3. 3 dc) in next ch-3 sp. Ch 1. 3 dc in next ch-1 sp. Ch 1. Join with sl st to top of ch 3.

4th rnd: Sl st in each of next 2 dc and ch-1 sp. Ch 3 (counts as dc). 2 dc in same sp as last sl st. (Ch 1. 3 dc in next ch-1 sp) twice. Ch 1. (3 dc. Ch 3. 3 dc) in next corner ch-3 sp. (Ch 1. 3 dc in next ch-1 sp) twice. Ch 1. (3 dc. Ch 3. 3 dc) in next corner ch-3 sp. (Ch 1. 3 dc in next ch-1 sp) 5 times. Ch 1. (3 dc. Ch 3. 3 dc) in next corner ch-3 sp. (Ch 1. 3 dc in next ch-1 sp) twice. (3 dc. Ch 3. 3 dc) in next corner ch-3 sp. (Ch 1. 3 dc in next ch-1 sp) twice. Join A with sl st to top of ch 3.

Cont in rnds as before, working (Ch 1. 3 dc) in ch-1 sps and (3 dc. Ch 3. 3 dc) in corner ch-3 sps, working 2 rnds each in A and B until shorter side of Blanket measures approx. 56" [142 cm]. Fasten off.

Abbreviations

Approx Approximately

Ch Chain(s)

Cont Continue

Dc Double crochet

Rnd Round(s)

RS Right side

Sl st Slip stitch

Sp(s) Space(s)

# Cinnamon Spice Granny Square Blanket

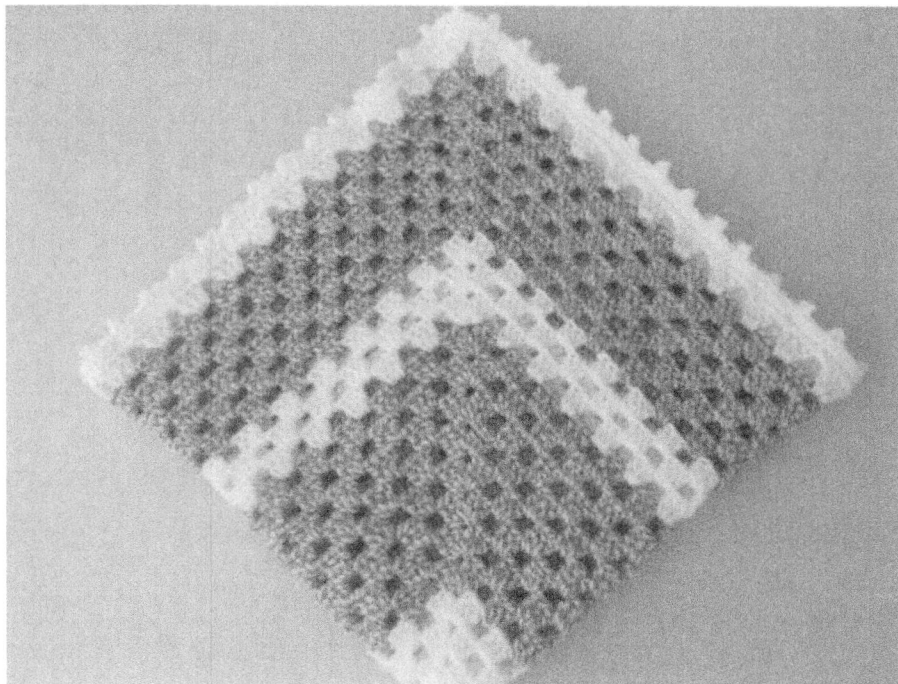

Size:     small for new born to 3 months baby

Gauge:   Length x width = 27 inches

16 to 20 stitches = 4 inches

Item to be need:

Two colors (cream and shaded light brown) worsted yarn 4ply

Crochet needle

Hook size. 3mm / US D 3.25mm

## ABBREVIATIONS:

c.      Crochet

ch.     Chain

sc      Single crochet

dc.     Double crochet

sts.    Stitches

st.     Stitch

slst    Slip stitches

sp      Space

Special st:    picot st:   make a single crochet stitch, make ch3, and slip stitch into the Front two loops in the same single crochet.

Pattern:

First make a magic circle.

Rnd1:   into the magic circle, ch3 (count as dc), 2dc, ch2, 3dc, repeat (3dc, ch2,

3dc) total (4 times), at the end slst to join in top of ch3, slst in next 2 sts,

slst into the next corner sp.(see pic )

Note: remember always starts a new round into the corner.

If you want to changing Colors don't slst into 2sts, only slst

at the end, cut the yarn. And then join a new color.

Rnd2:    into the corner, (ch3 (count as dc), 2dc, ch2, 3dc), ch2, work into

      the next corner, (3dc, ch2, 3dc),ch2, repeat [(3dc, ch2, 3dc),ch2]

      around,total (4 times), at the end slst to join in top of ch3, slst in next

      2 sts, slst into the next corner sp.(see pic )

Rnd3:   into the corner, (ch3 (count as dc), 2dc, ch2, 3dc), ch2, 3dc into next

ch2 space, Work into next corner, (3dc, ch2, 3dc), repeat [(3dc, ch2,

3dc, into corner),ch2, 3dc in next ch2 space] around, total (4 times) at

the end slst to join in top of ch3, slst in next 2 sts, slst into the next

corner sp.(see pic )

Rnd4:    into the corner, (ch3 (count as dc), 2dc, ch2, 3dc), ch2, 3dc into next ch2

space, ch2, 3dc in next ch2 space, ch2, Work into next corner, (3dc, ch2,

3dc), repeat [(3dc, ch2, 3dc, into corner),ch2, 3dc in next ch2 space,ch2,

3dc in next ch2 space, ch2], around total (4 times), at the end slst to join

in top of ch3, slst in next 2 sts, slst into the next corner sp.(see pic)

Rnd5-23: continue the pattern to the end.

Note: when you change the next color, always change

the Color after the joining, don't slst into 2sts, only slst

at the end of the round, cut the yarn. And then join a

new color, continue work as you want to large the size of

the blanket.

Rnd24:    ch1, sc into same st, sc in next 3dc sts, 2sc into ch2 space, repeat

(sc into 3dc sts, 2sc into ch2 space) at the end slst to join.

Make the edges:

Rnd25:    ch1, sc into same st, make a picot st (ch3 slst into same sc front 2loops),

sc into next 3sts,repeat [(sc into next st and make a picot st ch3 slst into same

sc front 2loops),sc in next 3sts], around the blanket. fasten off

Printed in Great Britain
by Amazon